S

HERE COME THE KILLER BEES

LAURENCE PRINGLE

William Morrow and Company, Inc.　　　New York

PHOTO CREDITS: Permission for the following photographs is gratefully acknowledged: Agricultural Research Service, USDA, p. 46; Beekeeping Education Service, Cheshire, CT, pp. 8 (© 1978 Ray Williamson, from "Life History and Activities of the Honeybee"), 11 and 48 (© 1984 Ray Williamson, from "The Amazing World of the Honeybee"), 13 and 21 (© 1984 Dewey M. Caron, from "The Africanized Honeybee in the Americas"); California Department of Food and Agriculture, pp. vi, 5 (both), 28, 36, 38; Troy Fore, Jr., *The Speedy Bee*, pp. 18, 23, 40, 44; Norman E. Gary, p. 4; Gard Otis, p. 33; Orley Taylor, p. 16 (left); G. F. Townsend, pp. 16 (right), 17; Mark Winston, p. 25.

Library of Congress Cataloging-in-Publication Data
Pringle, Laurence P.
  Here come the killer bees.
  Bibliography: p.
  Includes index.
  Summary: Describes the characteristics and behavior of
Africanized bees and discusses how they came to Brazil,
how they are spreading northward, and their potentially
disruptive influence on the native honeybee population
which in turn could damage crop yields and the honey and
beeswax industry.
  1. Brazilian honeybee—Juvenile literature.
[1. Brazilian honeybee.   2. Bees]   I. Title.
QL568.A6P76   1986   595.79'9   86-8499
ISBN 0-688-04630-4
ISBN 0-688-04631-2 (lib. bdg.)

CONTENTS

*The author wishes to thank Dr. Orley R. Taylor, Depart-
ment of Entomology—Snow Entomological Museum, The
University of Kansas, for reading the manuscript of this
book and helping to improve its accuracy.*

"The Africanized bee problem is real. It is rich with biological, economic, social, and political complications. It will be with us for a long time."

Dr. Orley Taylor
Department of Entomology
University of Kansas

from *Science* magazine,
October 17, 1980

With its tongue protruding, a young killer bee hatches from its cell. This bee was one of thousands found and killed in California in 1985.

1
HERE COMES TROUBLE

The first killer bee attack witnessed in the United States occurred early on June 6, 1985. That morning, oil company employee Bill Wilson drove a front-loader vehicle through a central California oil field called the Lost Hills site. Beside the road he noticed the dead bodies of a fox and a raven.

"I thought that was strange," Wilson recalls. "Still, I went ahead and worked. But at nine o'clock we get a break, and I went back over to look at the fox and the raven. As I drove up to where I'd seen them, I scared a rabbit out of the brush. Then these bees just swarmed out of this hole in the ground—it was a hole about eight, ten inches in diameter—and attacked the rabbit.

"Those bees just covered that rabbit, until I couldn't even see him. All I could see was his ears. . . . I don't think it was more than thirty to forty-five seconds—that rabbit was *dead*.

"Once he was dead, the bees headed straight for my loader—not just the five or six hundred on the rabbit, but a whole bunch more of 'em flew out; at least five, six thousand. Then they were all over the windows of the loader, all of those bees buzzing around out there, trying to get at me."

Fortunately, all the windows were closed and the bees did not reach Wilson. They gradually left the vehicle as he drove about a fifth of a mile from their nest. With the loader he then scooped up a half ton of oil-soaked soil, drove back, and dumped it on the hole as thousands of bees tried in vain to sting him.

Two weeks later, responding to Wilson's report of the incident, state animal control investigators found and killed about fifty bees that were still alive in the nest. The dead bees from Lost Hills were sent to a state laboratory in Sacramento for identification, but weren't examined for three weeks. When the bees finally were identified, they suddenly became a matter of great concern. Specimens were rushed to a federal bee research laboratory in Louisiana to confirm the identification. The answer came swiftly: that rabbit and Bill Wilson had been attacked by so-called killer bees.

Descendants of bees from Africa, these honeybees

2

have spread outward from Brazil since their accidental release there in 1957. Their fame also spread, as newspapers and other media described swarms of these bees stinging and sometimes killing people, livestock, and other animals. No wonder the term "killer bee" caught on with the public.

Entomologists, scientists who study insects, prefer to call them *Africanized bees* or simply *African bees.* They also are worried about these bees, but not because of the threat of stinging attacks on unwary people. That threat, in fact, has been greatly exaggerated. More realistically, Africanized bees could disrupt the entire honey and beeswax industry of the United States. Even worse, they could reduce the yield of many agricultural crops that are now pollinated by other varieties of honeybees.

Upon learning of the Lost Hills colony, a swarm of entomologists descended upon California. They were determined to learn how the bees had reached California and whether the subspecies had already established a foothold in the state.

The first question was easily answered. The bees had been found in an oil field, and there already were several known instances of Africanized bee nests being transported by ships carrying oil drilling pipe and other equipment from South America. Most likely, the Lost Hills bees had arrived that way. In 1984 a nest of Africanized bees had also reached the port of Oswego, New York, on Lake Ontario, aboard a freighter that had passed through the St. Lawrence Seaway. As a result of such incidents, the United States Department of Agriculture ordered a check on bee populations near forty ports visited by ships from Latin America.

When entomologists excavated the Lost Hills bee nest, they uncovered a chamber that once had been a fox den. Twenty honeycombs occupied a space 5½ feet long and a foot wide. Judging from the size of the nest and the darkly stained combs, the bees may have lived there for more than two years. The nest contained thousands of

At Lost Hills, California, entomologist Norman E. Gary examines the excavated site of the first Africanized bee nest found in the United States.

dead bees that probably had been suffocated by Wilson's actions. Entomologists also found three cells from which queen bees had emerged. It seemed likely that one or two queens and their swarms had left the nest before it was discovered.

A panel of entomologists and agricultural experts set up a plan to seek and destroy the Africanized bees. First, a special laboratory for identifying bees was established. To the casual observer, Africanized honeybees look like

In 1985, sample honeybees from thousands of colonies were collected and their wings and other body parts measured in order to identify and destroy Africanized bees in California.

other honeybees, though they tend to be smaller than other varieties in the United States. They weigh a bit less and have shorter tongues and forewings, but no single physical characteristic is enough to tell Africanized bees from other honeybees. So far, the most reliable identification method requires twenty-five different body measurements. Feeding these data into a computer enables entomologists to identify correctly Africanized bees 99.5 percent of the time.

The California panel declared that any wild colonies of honeybees found within 50 miles of Lost Hills were to be destroyed, and all commercial hives within a 20-mile radius had to be tested for the presence of the alien bees. No honeybees within that radius could be moved until all Africanized bees were found and killed.

This proved to be a hardship for beekeepers, and one commercial beekeeper tried to break the quarantine, trucking hives to his honey-extraction plant, which lay 180 miles away. Fortunately, he was stopped, and then a colony of Africanized bees was found in one of his Lost Hills hives, just 2 miles from the fox burrow nest. By late summer of 1985, five other Africanized bee colonies had been discovered. Three were in natural sites, such as a hollow tree stump 7 miles from the Lost Hills nest, and four in managed hives, up to 30 miles outside the Lost Hills quarantine area.

An even larger area was temporarily quarantined, and entomologists continued to check thousands of hives for the presence of Africanized bees. The quarantine ended in early December 1985. In all, twelve swarms of the fierce bees had been found and destroyed. With great effort, the bees were eliminated from their foothold in California, but this brought only a temporary reprieve. Advancing swarms of this troublesome bee had reached Honduras in 1985. Spreading northward at a rate of 200 to 300 miles each year, they were expected to cross Mexico's southern border in 1986. Unless they were slowed or stopped, Africanized honeybees would reach the Texas border as early as 1988 and no later than 1990.

Scientists had studied these bees intensely for more than a decade. They hoped to learn something about the life or behavior of the bees that would lead to effective control of the insects, but no "magic bullet" was found. The accidental outbreak of the Africanized bees in California was a grim reminder that there was little time left in which to somehow keep the so-called killer bees from bringing havoc to beekeeping and agriculture in the United States.

A queen honeybee lowers her abdomen into a comb cell and lays an egg. By early summer, she may lay 2,000 eggs a day. She may produce a half million eggs in her lifetime.

2

CLIMATE SHAPED THEIR LIVES

"Honey maker" is the meaning of the Latin word *Apis,* the genus of insects we call honeybees. Around the world, all species and subspecies of *Apis* are alike in many ways. All honeybees are social insects that live in colonies of up to sixty thousand bees. Each colony has a single *queen.* She may live several years, and she lays all the eggs from which *drones* (males) and *workers* (infertile females) develop. Worker bees secrete wax and with it build thousands of hexagonal cells. In some cells, eggs are deposited and develop into young bees; in others, honey is stored.

Worker bees are also the honey makers. They sip nectar from flowers and in the process spread pollen from one blossom to another. This accidental pollination service is vital to the successful reproduction of many plants. Within the crop of a worker bee, nectar is partially digested into simple sugars and then regurgitated into the cells of the bee's nest.

When a honeybee colony grows too large for its nest space, a process called *swarming* often occurs. Its queen flies to a new nest site; she is accompanied by about half of the colony's drones and workers. A new queen soon hatches and stays with the bees that remain.

There is still doubt about whether honeybees originated in Asia or Africa, but entomologists agree that the original honeybees evolved into several species and subspecies as they spread through the Old World, adapting to new environments. Climate had a powerful effect on the evolution of honeybees.

To survive in Europe, bees adapted to a temperate climate—warm in summer, cold in winter. Nests inside well-insulated hollows help honeybees survive the winter. Within their shelters and near their stored honey, they form a *winter cluster*—a large, continually moving sphere. Because this activity requires energy, honeybees of temperate regions store lots of honey, some of which they consume in winter.

Climate also influenced the swarming behavior of honeybees that evolved in Europe. Honeybees that live in temperate regions usually swarm early and just once in the flowering season. This allows the colony time to gather and store enough honey for its vital winter rations.

All worker honeybees have the ability to sting in order to defend the colony's young and stored food. However, the varieties of bees that evolved in temperate regions did not often have to defend their nests. Snug in hollow trees or other protected cavities, they had few enemies. They stung bears that tried to steal their honey, but they were not nearly as quick to sting as, for example, the kind of wasps called yellow jackets, which live in less secure nests.

After domesticating honeybees in Europe, people began to crossbreed different varieties, trying to get the best characteristics for their purposes. They wanted bees that were good honey producers, resistant to disease, and easy to handle. Today the gentlest types of honeybees come from southern Europe. Queen bees of Italian origin are commonly advertised in beekeeping journals.

Worker honeybees do virtually all of their colony's work—building, cleaning, food getting, and defending.

Until 1621 no honeybees existed in North or South America. Then colonists brought hives on their sailing ships, and European varieties of honeybees have thrived since in the temperate climate of North America. They are kept in large commercial *apiaries* (a collection of hives) and by many thousands of amateur beekeepers. Honeybees also live in the wild, nesting in hollow trees and other natural shelters, just as their ancestors did long ago in Europe.

The origins of so-called killer bees lie in Africa, where honeybees faced very different conditions from those in Europe. Most of the continent has a tropical climate without a long cold season. Honeybees do not need to store honey for winter survival, nor do they need to nest inside trees for protection against cold. As a result, African bees build rather small nests that contain less honey than those of European honeybees.

Many colonies, especially in arid regions, make nests out in the open—on a tree branch or in a rocky crevice. This leaves the nest vulnerable to attack. For millions of years, African bees have contended with predators such as ants, honey badgers, and people. For their own protection, they became easily provoked and highly defensive, and only the most unapproachable colonies survived.

An alarm scent from one disturbed worker bee may trigger defensive action by hundreds or thousands of others. African bees respond more quickly, stay agitated longer, and chase enemies farther than European varieties of honeybees. The sting of an African bee is no

A colony of Africanized honeybees in Panama built this nest out in the open on a tree, as their relatives in Africa sometimes do.

more dangerous than that of other honeybees, but several hundred tiny doses of venom from any bee can be fatal.

The fierce temperament of African bees must always be kept in mind. In 1974 William Lyon, an American entomologist, taught at the University of Nairobi in Kenya. An amateur beekeeper in his home state of Ohio, Lyon had also successfully transferred swarms of wild African honeybees into hives at the university without mishap. One hive remained empty, and he was asked to investigate a colony living inside a wall of a new house in a nearby village. As long as the bees remained, the house couldn't be rented. Lyon and his assistant drove to the village. They donned hats, veils, gloves, and overalls, and they then urged the women and children of the village to stay back at least 40 to 50 yards.

Without warning, Lyon's assistant ripped some siding from the house. "That was the mistake!" Lyon wrote later. "Bees came boiling out of their nest literally by the thousands, swarming and stinging everything in sight. . . . The women, children, and livestock were soon reached. Most everyone seemed to be crying and screaming, covering their bodies with blankets. . . . The bees entered the huts by the hundreds, stinging old persons who were unaware of what was happening."

Bees crawled under Lyon's veil, stinging him on his ears, nose, cheeks, eyelids, and forehead. He wore low shoes, and was stung about fifty times on his ankles and lower legs. Lyon and his assistant ran to the car and jumped in, accompanied by several hundred bees.

Lyon and his assistant returned with insecticide and sprayed the nest area and some pigs and goats that were lying on the ground. Bees were still stinging anything that moved an hour and a half after they were disturbed. William Lyon feared that he had earned the hatred of the villagers, but later he learned that matters had ended well. Two goats and a chicken had died from stings, but all of the people had recovered. The bees fled, and so the house could be rented. Furthermore, from within the wall of the house, the villagers recovered two washtubs full of honey.

Because African honeybees do not need large stores of honey for winter, they are free to swarm more frequently than bees from a temperate climate. African bees use more cells for raising young than for honey storage. This causes a hive population to grow rapidly, setting the stage for swarming.

African bees are also quick to abandon a nest, which is called *absconding*. A fire near a nest or any other disturbance may cause the entire colony to flee. They abscond most frequently in the wet season, and also abscond at the end of a long dry season. Because winter cold does not loom ahead, African bees can abandon their combs and set off in search of a better nectar-foraging area. European honeybees rarely abscond, even when living in the tropics. For example, during the rainy season in French Guinea, when few plants bloom, colonies of European honeybees died out rather than abandon their hives.

Despite their tendencies to abscond and to sting, Af-

A swarm of Africanized bees rests on a tree in French Guinea (left). In Africa, many beekeepers use hives made of bark (center) or of hollow logs such as the ones shown hanging from a baobab tree (right).

rican honeybees are kept in great numbers by African people. In some parts of East Africa, more than half of the population keep honeybees. Most beekeepers use traditional native hives made of bark or hollow logs. They avoid disturbing their bees in daylight and usually remove honey and beeswax at night, when they suffer fewer stings. With primitive equipment and limited knowledge, their average yield is quite low—30 pounds of honey and 2 pounds of beeswax per year from a colony.

Some South African beekeepers run large commercial

apiaries. One beekeeper produces 80 tons of honey each year from fifteen hundred bee colonies. To replace colonies that abscond, the keeper sets out hives along routes commonly traveled by swarming bees. In one year he caught more than seven hundred colonies in this way. To counter the fierce defensive behavior of the bees, up to sixty hives are kept inside specially designed houses in which people can work safely without being stung much. Thus, when people have an understanding of the bees and are able to make or buy the right equipment, they can extract a bounty of honey and beeswax from African bees.

17

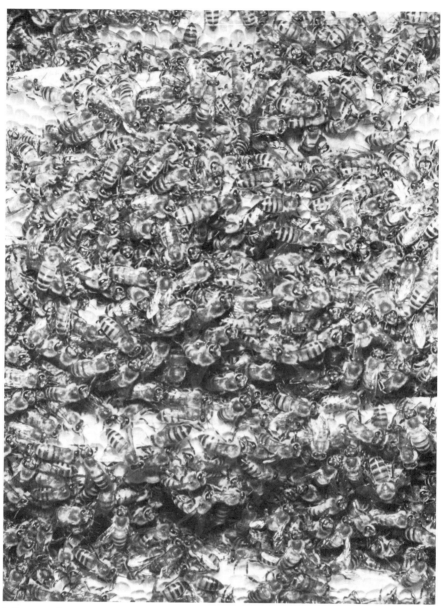

These Africanized bees photographed in Venezuela are descendants of the African queen bees that escaped in Brazil.

3
BIRTH OF A LEGEND

For more than a century, beekeepers in Africa and in South America imported European honeybees, but these temperate-zone bees did not fare well in much of the tropics. In the 1950s, the Brazilian government tried to find ways to boost national honey production. One step was to support bee breeding research by geneticist Warwick Kerr at the University of São Paulo.

Kerr knew that African honeybees could be good honey producers, so in 1956 he imported a number of African queens in order to conduct some captive cross-breeding experiments. He also knew of the savage reputation of African bees and of the potential folly in releasing an alien organism into a new environment. This often has bad results, as demonstrated by destruction caused by gypsy moths, introduced to North America, and by European rabbits, introduced to Australia.

Kerr took special precautions to prevent escape of the queen bees. Each hive had an *excluder,* a special entrance cover—like a filter—that kept the large queens inside. As the queens reproduced offspring, the cover kept the even larger drones inside, too, but allowed the small worker bees to pass in and out. Thus, the workers were free to bring nectar and pollen to the hive, but queens and drones could not escape to reproduce.

Kerr's research had barely begun in 1957 when a visiting beekeeper mistakenly removed the queen excluders. Twenty-six queens and their swarms of drones and workers escaped before the mistake was discovered. African honeybees were loose in Brazil.

They soon demonstrated their superiority to temperate zone bees in a tropical environment. European races never had established much of a feral population in Latin America, as they commonly do in cooler climates. (Domesticated animals gone wild and their descendents are called *feral*.) The African queens and their swarms readily nested in the wild. Reproducing quickly and swarming frequently, African honeybees began to spread in all directions.

The African bees overwhelmed European bees kept in apiaries. In some areas, they robbed hives of honey or took over hives, killing the less aggressive occupants. African drones mated with European queens, and the following generations, called *Africanized bees,* retained the aggressiveness of their fathers. Their savage defensiveness surprised and alarmed Brazilians. In Brazil, as in other Latin American countries, most bee hives were kept near homes and roads, close to where people live and travel. People were accustomed to the presence of docile European honeybees. Suddenly they found that a slight disturbance sparked stinging attacks by hundreds of bees.

In Latin America, most apiaries were located near roads, homes, or places where livestock was kept—all places where the highly defensive Africanized bees might be disturbed.

A few horrifying incidents, given wide publicity, helped create the legend of the killer bees. One man was found dead with a thousand stings on his head; he had shot himself to end his agony. Another man, on horseback, collided with a swarm of Africanized bees. The horse threw him to the ground, breaking the man's leg, and then ran off with the bees in pursuit. Three days later the horse died from the countless stings it had received.

In 1975 a teacher named Dr. Eglantina Portugal passed near a swarm of Africanized bees as she approached her school in the city of Aracaju, Brazil. One bee stung her, and she slapped it. The bee released its alarm scent, and a witness described what followed:

"Suddenly hundreds, thousands of bees appeared. Dr. Eglantina ran, but she had a lame leg. She tripped and fell into a ditch. She crawled out. I could see many bees on her face and neck. More bees were coming all the time.

"I wanted to help, but it was impossible to leave my closed car; bees were all over it. Some people from nearby houses arrived with water, but the bees stung them and drove them back. Finally firemen arrived, but they, too, ran away with bees all over them. They returned waving smoking torches and were able to get Dr. Eglantina to the hospital. But it was too late."

Exactly why people die from many bee stings is not known. Some are allergic to bee venom; for them, one sting can be fatal. For others, massive stinging seems to cause heart or kidney failure, but there are other causes of death from many bee stings and more knowledge is needed in order to develop effective medical treatment.

Each year brings new reports of attacks by Africanized bees. In 1983, for example, a swarm stung residents of a Brazilian nursing home, killing one woman and injuring twenty-two other elderly people. Many unfortunate hens and goats also have died. Alarming though such incidents are, they give a false impression of Africanized bees. First, they sting only to defend their hive or swarm. Second, stinging incidents involving large numbers of bees are not common. They kill many fewer people than sensational stories in newspapers, magazines, and other media would have you believe.

Stinging incidents follow patterns. Most occur during the honeybee swarming season. Also, most fatalities occur during the first four years after Africanized bees invade a region. After that period, most people learn to avoid encounters with the bees, and the number of deaths from stings declines. Another factor that affects deaths caused by bees is the density of the human and bee

"Don't Attack the Africanized Bees" warns a poster in Panama. Once people learn to avoid the bees, stinging incidents decrease.

population. Wherever both people and Africanized bees are abundant, a certain number of stinging incidents is inevitable, and some people die.

Accurate data on bee sting deaths in Latin America are difficult to obtain. The number varies from year to year and sometimes totals only a dozen. In contrast, European honeybees in the United States kill at least forty people a year—twice as many as are killed by venomous snakes. Most victims are allergic to bee venom and die from just one sting. Thus, the comparatively docile European honeybee might be considered as deserving of the term killer bee as the Africanized honeybee.

Even though their killer reputation has been exaggerated, Africanized bees have driven thousands of Latin American beekeepers out of business. As the bees spread outward from southeastern Brazil, they took over all existing colonies of European honeybees. Their tendency to sting and abscond readily discouraged most beekeepers.

In Brazil more than half of all beekeepers abandoned or destroyed their apiaries. The same occurred in other nations as Africanized honeybees moved southwest into Paraguay and Argentina, west into Bolivia and Peru, and north into Surinam, Venezuela, Colombia, and beyond. Honey production fell. Venezuela, for example, had a harvest of 578 tons of honey in 1975. Africanized bees reached Venezuela in 1977, and by 1981 the honey harvest had fallen to 100 tons.

In 1984 Dr. Orley "Chip" Taylor, entomologist at the University of Kansas and an authority on Africanized

Soon after Africanized bees reached Costa Rica, this apiary was abandoned by its owner.

bees, reported in the *American Bee Journal* that "Bee-keeping still appears to be severely depressed in Paraguay, Uruguay, Bolivia, Surinam, Guyana, Venezuela, and is presently declining in Peru, Ecuador, Colombia, and Trinidad. Declines in production should also soon be evident in Panama and Costa Rica."

From southern Brazil, however, came reports of increasing honey production and of beekeepers who praised the bees they used to curse. After a difficult period of adjustment, commercial beekeepers had a better understanding of Africanized bees and were learning to manage them better. They were assisted financially and technically by the Brazilian government.

Respecting the famed defensiveness of the bees, keepers moved hives more than 600 feet from homes and livestock. (Hives could be closer if bushes and trees screened the bees from potential disturbance.) Individual hives were set farther apart than before, and beekeepers learned to move quietly and slowly near their bees. Veils, bee suits, and other protective wear proved to be vital, though uncomfortable in the tropics.

If a colony was especially aggressive, beekeepers removed its queen, replacing it with the daughter of a queen of a less defensive colony. Such colonies became less aggressive and usually were also good honey producers. To keep Africanized bees from absconding, keepers fed colonies when flower nectar was scarce and also made sure there was plenty of hive space. (A sense of becoming crowded, or running out of space, stimulates swarming behavior in honeybees.)

Brazilian beekeepers began to view Africanized bees as an asset instead of a problem. In one area, European bees in an apiary produced just 20 pounds of honey in a month and a half, whereas Africanized bees in the same apiary produced 77 pounds in that time. Brazilian beekeepers also discovered that honey could be produced in northeastern Brazil, a region where European honeybees had failed to survive. The climate of northeastern Brazil is like that of the semi-arid regions of Africa where African bees thrive. The existence of feral colonies of Africanized bees also provided some peasants a new kind of livelihood as hunters of wild honey.

The glowing reports from Brazil seemed to contradict everything people had heard about Africanized bees. Would honey production also rebound in other Latin

American nations? In 1984 Dr. Orley Taylor offered his opinion: "In my view the recovery of the industry in Southern Brazil is the exception and not the rule."

He warned that recovery in other countries would come only from training of beekeepers and changes in their attitudes. He also questioned whether Africanized bees are really superior to European bees throughout the tropics. In the dry habitat of western Venezuela, European bees used to produce 100 to 200 pounds of honey per hive in a year. As they foraged near their apiaries, these bees had no competition from feral honeybees.

Now there is a large feral population of Africanized bees that competes for nectar with bees from apiaries. Whether beekeepers have European or Africanized bees in their hives, they seldom get more than 65 pounds of honey a year. The beekeepers are trying to survive on a third of the honey they once harvested while faced with greater costs of managing the Africanized bees. "It is worth remembering," wrote Orley Taylor, "that the so-called 'superior' honey production by African bees has put many beekeepers out of business."

By foraging for food while in the swarming stage, Africanized bees obtain energy that enables them to travel many miles before settling into a new nest.

4

SWARMING NORTHWARD

As Africanized bees swarmed northward toward the Texas border, the United States Department of Agriculture supported many studies of the insects. One investigator, Dr. Orley "Chip" Taylor, traveled widely in Latin America to chart the movements of the bees and to predict how fast and far they would spread.

He collected honeybees from flowers, colonies, food markets, and sugar processing plants. He also spoke with beekeepers, government officials, and ordinary citizens. Dead bees that he collected had to be measured carefully in order to identify them correctly, but Dr.

Taylor found that he could recognize live bees by their behavior. Africanized bees were more nervous than European bees within their hives and at their entrances. In flight, Africanized honeybees moved more rapidly and in a more noticeable zigzag motion than European bees.

Dr. Taylor found that Africanized honeybees spread most rapidly in dry habitats, especially coastal savannas (areas of grassland, scattered trees, and small patches of forest). This habitat is similar to that in East Africa, where African honeybees thrive. The bees advanced more slowly through the interior rain forest.

In their first few years in Brazil, the range of Africanized bees expanded outward about 50 miles a year. By 1963 large numbers of colonies had been established, and the bees' range began to increase dramatically through dry regions. Now the bees advanced at a pace of 300 miles a year.

This astonished people who knew only European bees. According to the most detailed study of European swarms, bees scouting for a new nest site fly up to 2.7 miles, but their swarms usually settle into a nest within a mile of their former home. No one knows how far, on the average, swarms of Africanized bees travel before renesting. (Swarming bees *do* pause to rest and sometimes to feed.) Their African ancestors reportedly have flown nearly a hundred miles. Africanized bees have established populations on islands that are separated from the South American mainland by 14 miles of open ocean. A Brazilian beekeeper claimed that he followed, by car and bicycle, a swarm of bees a distance of 175 miles.

Thus, with each colony able to produce a new swarm just fifty days after nesting, Africanized bees clearly are able to occupy new territory at a dizzying pace.

Based on his findings in Latin America, Orley Taylor in 1975 assumed that Africanized honeybees would move northward at a rate of 200 to 300 miles each year. The bees have stayed on schedule. Taylor also tried to determine how far north in the northern hemisphere these tropical insects could survive. Some clues came from the distribution of the African honeybee on its native continent and from the range of Africanized bees in Argentina. Both Africa and Argentina are in the southern hemisphere, so the farther south the bees range, the cooler the climate.

In South Africa honeybees can live up to 60 days a year at temperatures in the range of 62 to 39 degrees Fahrenheit (17 to 4 degrees Celsius). They also survive a similar period with freezing temperatures. They experience a 215-day growing season—the span between the first and last frosts of a year. The length of the growing season is vital to honeybees, because the killing frost that marks its end halts their food-gathering from flowers. Early reports from southern and western Argentina suggested that Africanized honeybees starved for lack of flowers rather than died from extreme cold.

In 1975 it appeared to Orley Taylor that the length of the growing season might be a more vital survival factor than cold temperatures. Applying this information to the climate of the United States, he predicted that Africanized bees would occupy approximately the lower

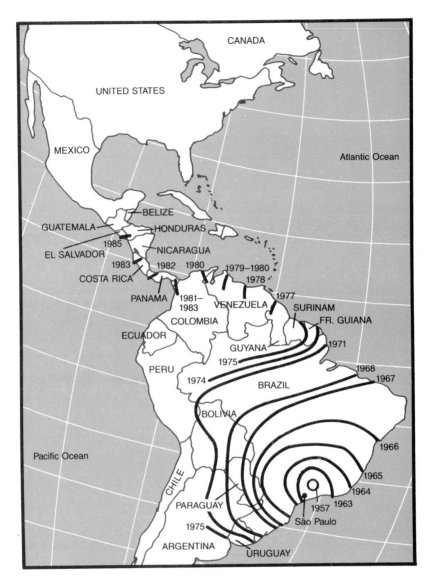

Africanized bees rapidly expanded their range after twenty-six queens escaped near São Paulo, Brazil, in 1957. They reached Honduras in 1985 and are expected to invade southern Mexico in 1986 and the United States a few years later.

Dr. Orley "Chip" Taylor began studying Africanized bees in 1974. Here he weighs a colony of the bees, which are docile because they are in the swarming stage and are well-fed.

quarter of the nation. He drew climatic lines on a map of the United States that he believed might represent the bees' distribution. One line marked areas having a growing season of 240 days. Taylor assumed that Africanized honeybees would thrive and establish permanent populations in regions having a growing season of 240 or more days. If so, the bees would live as far north as San Francisco on the West Coast and up to southeastern Maryland on the East Coast, but not nearly that far north in the center of the United States.

By the early 1980s the southern limits of the Africanized bees' range were more clearly defined. Surveys in Argentina showed how the success of the bees declined as they spread into cooler climates. In a zone that includes Argentina's capital, Buenos Aires, the bees established colonies in the growing season but failed to survive most winters.

North of that zone the bees lived year around. A key difference between the two areas seemed to be the mean (average) high temperature of the coldest month, which is July in Argentina. Africanized bees died in places where the mean maximum temperature in July was below 60 degrees (F) or 16 degrees (C). They survived if the mean maximum was 60 degrees (F) or above.

Orley Taylor and his colleague at the University of Kansas, Marla Spivak, decided that the 60 degree (F) line in January—the coldest month in the United States— would be the best predictor of the northern limit of

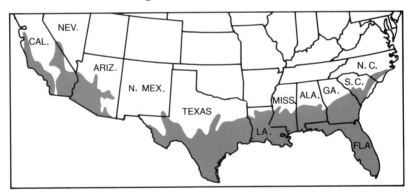

Africanized bees will probably live year-round in the region shown in gray, and farther north in summertime and during years having mild winters.

Africanized bees. The map on page 34 shows the border line, which extends up to Santa Cruz, California (south of San Francisco), on the West Coast and near Fayetteville, North Carolina, on the East. The bees could colonize the area from Texas to North Carolina in eight years if people did nothing to stop them.

South of the line on the map the climate is even warmer. Nearly all of Florida, for example, has a mean high temperature in January of 66 degrees (F) or 19 degrees (C). In such a climate, Africanized bees have been highly successful, making up all captive and feral colonies. It seems likely that they will also thrive and replace European honeybees in the warmest parts of the United States' Sunbelt. These include nearly all of Florida, and southern parts of Georgia, Mississippi, Louisiana, Texas, Arizona, and California.

In somewhat colder regions of the United States, Africanized bees and European bees will probably co-exist, as they do in parts of Argentina. In still colder areas, where the mean high temperature in January is below 60 degrees (F), Africanized bees still may appear in the summer as they swarm northward or are spread accidentally by people. Mild winters will enable them to survive for a while beyond their usual overwintering zone. Harsh winters will wipe out these northern outposts.

Most of the United States and all of Canada will be spared the permanent presence of Africanized honeybees. Nevertheless, they will have a far-reaching impact. First, they will reduce honey harvests wherever

A European honeybee pollinates a flower—an act we pay little attention to but which is worth an estimated $8 billion a year to United States agriculture.

they can survive year around. Many thousands of amateurs who keep a few hives in their backyard will have to give up their hobby because of the aggressiveness of the bees unless they learn to keep European rather than African bees in their colonies. Second, and more serious by far, will be the Africanized bees' effect on firms that raise queen bees for sale.

More than 90 percent of all queen rearing in the United States occurs within the zone where Africanized bees can survive in all seasons. Many beekeepers replace queen bees annually to ensure high honey yields from their colonies. Each spring young queens are shipped to thousands of beekeepers all over the United States and Canada. These beekeepers will not want queens that have mated with Africanized drones. So the people who raise queens must somehow keep Africanized drones from mating with their European queens. Failing that, they will have to relocate their businesses to northern sites beyond the reach of Africanized bees.

One way or another, Africanized bees will reduce the nation's honey and beeswax production, worth $150 million a year. That sum is dwarfed by the value of European honeybees as pollinators. Their value to United States agriculture is estimated at $8 *billion*. Honeybees account for about 80 percent of all insect pollination of agricultural crops in the United States. Their pollination is vital to ninety vegetable, fruit, seed, and nut crops, including cucumbers, muskmelons, oranges, nectarines, peaches, apples, cherries, alfalfa, and almonds.

Some of this vital pollination is done for free by bees from feral colonies or from hives of the nation's two hundred thousand beekeeping hobbyists. West of the Mississippi, however, most agricultural pollination is done by bees provided by commercial bee-rearing firms, which transport honeybees from one flowering crop to the next. Each year, for example, six hundred thousand hives are trucked into California's almond orchards when the trees begin to flower. No honeybees, no almond crop. In California alone, honeybee pollination of

Commercial pollination services move bee hives from place to place as different crop plants come into flower.

almonds and fifty other crops is valued at $4 billion a year.

This pollination service will be disrupted by the presence of Africanized bees in the Sunbelt. One commercial beekeeper in California predicted a catastrophe, saying, "We beekeepers could gear up to handle them, but the irrigators, harvesters, and tractor drivers—the people who have to work in the fields—would have an awful time."

Most people in the United States will never encounter Africanized bees, but everyone may be stung by a scarcity of certain foods and with higher prices for some bee-pollinated agricultural products.

In a Mexican honey-processing plant, pieces of honeycomb are loaded into a machine that separates honey from beeswax. Mexico exports most of its honey to Europe.

5

CAN THEY BE TAMED?

The full impact of Africanized bees will not be known until the bees invade all suitable habitat in the United States. Meanwhile, entomologists expect answers to some of their questions about the bees as they move north through Mexico, a major honey producer and exporter.

Mexico's beekeepers take more than 146 million pounds of honey annually from more than 2½ million hives. Although honeybee management is primitive in some areas, especially the Yucatan Peninsula, many Mexican beekeepers use modern techniques and equipment with their European bees. Mexico's central high-lands are home to some of the world's largest beekeeping operations. The most skilled beekeepers rear queens for their own colonies and for sale to others. They also move hives to different localities to take advantage of varied flowering times.

Such beekeepers may be able to adjust to the presence of Africanized bees. Judging from results south of Mexico, however, most amateur beekeepers and poorly trained commercial beekeepers will be driven from business by Africanized bees. One source of trouble lies in the intense nature of beekeeping in Mexico. In some regions apiaries occupy every available site. Many are located close to people and livestock, and there will be no places to relocate them away from potential disturbance when Africanized bees take over.

The Mexican government has tried to prepare its beekeepers and the public for life with Africanized bees, but this is a formidable and expensive task. One vital factor in managing hives of Africanized bees is the ability to replace their queens with queens of docile European varieties, but imported queens are too costly for most Mexican beekeepers. Mexico needs to produce two million of its own European queens annually and also teach inexperienced beekeepers how to requeen their colonies. Mexican beekeepers also need bee suits, veils, and large smoke-producing devices (smoke calms honeybees and Africanized bees usually require heavy doses). The cost of this gear also may be beyond the means of many Mexican beekeepers.

Mexico was, of course, the last place where African-ized bees could be stopped from reaching the United States. For decades the goal of somehow blocking the northward march of the bees was wished for by many people and actively studied by a few. Some beekeepers once believed that the vast Amazonian rain forest would provide a natural barrier to Africanized bees. That failed, as did the hoped-for barrier of Panama's eastern rain forest. Had a method of stopping Africanized bees been ready, Panama, narrowest of Central American coun-tries, would have been the place to implement it. The bees swept through Panama during 1982–1983.

Defending the 1,300-mile border between Mexico and the United States against bees is out of the question; and any plan to block Africanized bees by simply finding and destroying their colonies will fail, considering the vast area that would have to be searched for the elusive bees. In December 1984, sixty beekeepers from the United States and Canada recommended that the United States Department of Agriculture (USDA) explore the feasibility of a barrier zone in Mexico. They had toured USDA research apiaries in Venezuela and reported that the undesirable characteristics of the African bee far ex-ceeded their expectations. They proposed that the bees be blocked in Mexico by several methods: saturation of the area with European drones that would mate with Africanized queens and pass their more desirable char-acteristics on to their young, placement of bait to lure wild bees into traps, destruction of feral colonies, and use of chemical or biological control agents.

Visiting Venezuela, beekeepers from North America found Africanized bees more troublesome than they expected. Here the bees attack a dark-colored camera strap.

Some of these ideas have merit and are being investigated by scientists. But the fast-moving Africanized bees left little time for action. By the mid-1980s entomologists had learned a great deal about Africanized bees, but they did not have enough knowledge to say, "This is it. Here's how to block those bees."

The answer to taming the bees seemed to lie in their

reproduction. Entomologists were particularly interested in understanding the natural crossbreeding between Africanized and European bees—and trying to influence it.

They had watched for evidence that Africanized bees had changed as a result of breeding with bees of European origin. From Latin America there had been some reports of tamer Africanized bees. To check these reports, the stinging behavior of Africanized bees was investigated in 1981 by Dr. Anita Collins and other entomologists from the USDA's Bee Breeding and Stock Center Laboratory in Louisiana. They compared the defensive behavior of European bees in Louisiana with that of Africanized bees in similar-sized colonies and with similar weather in Venezuela.

The Africanized colonies always had more bees defending their hive entrances, ready to fly toward intruders, and they stung a leather target six to eight times as much as did European bees. Reporting their results in the journal *Science,* Anita Collins and her colleagues concluded: "This refutes the idea that the migrating bees have become milder through hybridization with 'native' bees."

After nearly thirty years in Latin America, Africanized bees did not differ significantly from their African ancestors that escaped in Brazil. (And so they are still called African bees by some entomologists.) The major reason for this lack of change was the lack of feral colonies of European bees. In Mexico, however, Africanized bees will encounter for the first time an abundant, vigorous

Smoke was used to calm Africanized bees in Venezuela after Dr. Anita Collins and other scientists tested their defensive behavior. The bees stung targets six to eight times more than European honeybees.

wild population of European bees, as well as a large domesticated one. Entomologists will watch for signs of change in Africanized bees. If European honeybees can be Africanized, can Africanized bees be European-ized? Might they develop more desirable traits as they interbreed with the gentle European bees?

The answer is probably no, because differences in the natural mating patterns of the two bees may put European honeybees at a disadvantage. Queens mate while flying a mile or more from their colonies, pursued by drones from other colonies. A queen mates with from seven to seventeen drones and then returns to her nest with enough sperm cells for a lifetime of egg laying.

Drones from a queen's colony usually do not fly as far as the queen, and this allows drones from other colonies to mate with her. In most of Latin America this meant that European queen bees mated mostly with the abundant Africanized drones. No wonder the colonies of European bees became Africanized so swiftly. In Mexico and the United States, however, both European queens and Africanized queens on their mating flights will have a greater chance of mating with the plentiful European drones.

Africanized bees, however, have one other mating advantage over European bees. Their queens and drones take mating flights late in the afternoon, after most European drones return to their colonies. This helps to ensure that the queens mate mostly with Africanized drones and that their offspring retain the characteristics of Africanized bees. The only way to defeat this mating

The full impact of Africanized bees on the United States will not be known until after the year 2000, but they seem sure to cause trouble in the 1990s.

advantage is to develop populations of European bees that have late-flying drones.

This goal is not so far-fetched, and it is being pursued by Drs. Orley Taylor and Gareth Rowell of the University of Kansas. In 1983 they began observing the flight times of European drones from many different colonies. There *were* a variety of "flight schedules," including some that lasted into late afternoon. In 1984 they began a breeding program aimed at producing a population of European honeybees with this late-flying drone characteristic. If developed, these bees could gradually replace existing European colonies in Mexico and the southern United States. European drones would then be able to compete with Africanized drones, mate with Africanized queens, and pass some of their characteristics on to the queens' young. With their greater numbers, the European bees could then tame the alien bees by reproducing with them.

If European honeybees can be given a mating advantage over Africanized bees, the future of beekeeping, of honey production, and of many agricultural crops in the United States will look brighter. For now, the outlook remains cloudy as the bees swarm nearer and nearer.

FOR YOUR SAFETY

Although so-called killer bees are not a major health hazard, precautions should be taken if you live or visit within their range. Remember, the bees do not seek victims but do defend their colonies and swarms aggressively. Therefore, for your own safety:

- Keep several hundred feet away from honeybee hives or swarms, and avoid disturbing them in any way.
- Be alert to accidental encounters with flying or resting swarms of Africanized bees. In the United States their peak swarming season will be in the summer months.
- If Africanized bees start to sting, release penned animals so they can escape. A person can usually outdistance the bees with a quick run of 150 feet or more. If there is no building or other shelter available, flee behind shrubs, trees, or other obstacles that block the bees' line of vision.
- For most people a few bee stings cause no more harm than painful swelling. However, anyone who has been stung and who feels dizzy or has difficulty breathing, or who has been stung fifty times or more, should be treated by a doctor as soon as possible.

GLOSSARY

abscond—to leave quickly and secretly. Swarms of African honeybees abscond frequently, a characteristic that makes them more difficult to manage than European varieties of honeybees.

allergy—an especially sensitive or extreme reaction to an environmental factor or substance in amounts that do not affect most people. People who are allergic to bee venom can die from a single sting.

apiary—a place where honeybee colonies are kept in a collection of hives and raised for their honey.

drone—the male honeybee, which does not work and lacks a sting. Drones live from late spring to the end of the summer. Their role is to mate with a queen, and their large eyes are an adaptation for seeing a queen bee on her mating flight. Drones die soon after mating.

entomology—the scientific study of insects.

evolution—the process by which the characteristics of a population or entire species of organisms gradually change over a period of time.

genetics—the study of the heredity of living things, or how parents pass characteristics on to their offspring.

growing season—the frost-free span of time in a year. Northern regions have shorter growing seasons than southern areas, and this climatic factor affects where different kinds of plants and animals can live.

hybrid—the offspring produced by breeding plants or animals of different varieties, such as two varieties of honeybees.

hybridization—the process of producing hybrids.

pollen—the male sex cells of flowering plants.

pollination—the process of conveying or transferring pollen from an anther to a stigma of a flower. When male sex cells (pollen grains) reach female sex cells, fertilization occurs. The fertilized eggs then develop into seeds. In their quest for food, honeybees and other kinds of insects accidentally spread pollen around and play a vital role in pollination.

quarantine—the enforced isolation or restriction of movement that is imposed in order to prevent the spread of a disease or other harmful agent. In 1985 a quarantine on movement of honeybee colonies was part of a successful strategy to find and destroy colonies of Africanized honeybees in California.

queen—the sexually fertile female that is the heart of a colony of social bees, including honeybees. A queen honeybee may live for several years, during which she can lay a million eggs. The fertilized eggs she lays develop into worker bees or queens (one of which will eventually replace her); unfertilized eggs develop into drones.

species—a population or many populations of an organism that have characteristics in common, which make them different from individuals of other populations. The members of a species interbreed with each other but not with members of other species. Thus, different populations of honeybees interbreed, but honeybees cannot interbreed with other bee species.

swarm—a group of honeybees, with its queen, emigrating to a new nest site. Usually at least half of a colony's workers and drones accompany a queen. Before swarming the bees fill themselves with honey, for they usually go without food until scout bees locate a new home.

worker—the infertile female bee that does virtually all work in a honeybee colony. Workers are the builders, cleaners, nurses, honey makers, and defenders of their colony.

FURTHER READING

Anonymous. *Final Report: Committee on the African Honeybee.* Washington, D.C.: National Academy of Sciences, 1972.

Bradbear, Nocola, and DeJong, David. *The Management of Africanized Honeybees.* Leaflet #2, International Bee Research Association.

Collins, Anita, *et al.* "Colony Defense by Africanized and European Honey Bees." *Science,* October 1, 1982, pp. 72–74.

DeJong, David. "Africanized Bees Now Preferred by Brazilian Beekeepers." *American Bee Journal,* February 1984, pp. 116–118. (See also a response to this article: Taylor, Orley. "Challenges Africanized Bee Article." *American Bee Journal,* May 1984, pp. 395–396.)

Fore, Troy. "Group of Beekeepers Visits Venezuela to Experience African Bees First Hand." *The Speedy Bee,* August 1985, pp. 9–14.

Garelik, Glenn. "The Killers." *Discover,* October 1985, pp. 108–115.

Gore, Rick. "Those Fiery Brazilian Bees." *National Geographic,* April 1976, pp. 491–501.

Longgood, William. *The Queen Must Die, and Other Affairs of Bees and Men.* New York: W. W. Norton & Company, 1985.

Lyon, William F. "My Experience With the African Honeybee." *Gleanings in Bee Culture,* November 1974, pp. 335–336.

Morse, Roger. *The Complete Guide to Beekeeping.* New York: E.P. Dutton, 1974.

Rinderer, T., and Sylvester, H. A. "Identification of Africanized Bees." *American Bee Journal,* July 1981, pp. 512–516.

Rinderer, T., *et al.* "Nectar-Foraging Characteristics of Africanized and European Honeybees in the Neotropics." *Journal of Apicultural Research,* Vol. 23, no. 2 (1984), pp. 70–79.

Rinderer, T., *et al.* "Size of Nest Cavities Selected by Swarms of Africanized Honeybees in Venezuela." *Journal of Apicultural Research,* Vol. 20, no. 3 (1981), pp. 160–164.

Taylor, Orley. "African Bees: Potential Impact in the United States." *Bulletin of the Entomological Society of America,* Winter 1985, pp. 15–24.

Taylor, Orley. "Health Problems Associated with African Bees." *Annals of Internal Medicine,* February 1986, pp. 267–268.

Taylor, Orley. "Let's Keep Our Facts Straight About African Bees!". *American Bee Journal,* August 1985, pp. 586–587.

Taylor, Orley. "The Past and Possible Future Spread of Africanized Honeybees in the Americas." *Bee World,*

Vol. 58, no. 1 (1977), pp. 19–30.

Taylor, Orley, and Levin, M. D. "Observations of Africanized Honey Bees Reported to South and Central American Government Agencies." *Bulletin of the Entomological Society of America,* Vol. 24, no. 4 (1978), pp. 412–414.

Taylor, Orley, and Rowell, Gareth. "Feral Swarms Seen as Key to African Bee Control." *The Speedy Bee,* March 1985, p. 10.

Taylor, Orley, and Spivak, Marla. "Climatic Limits of Tropical African Honeybees in the Americas." *Bee World,* Vol. 65, no. 1 (1984), pp. 38–47.

Townsend, G. F. "Beekeeping in East Africa." *American Bee Journal,* November and December 1970, pp. 420–422 (November), pp. 462–463 (December).

Winston, Mark. "The Potential Impact of the Africanized Honey Bee on Apiculture in Mexico and Central America." *American Bee Journal,* August and September 1979, pp. 584–586 (August), pp. 642–645 (September).

Winston, Mark, *et al.* "Absconding Behavior of the Africanized Honeybee in South America." *Journal of Apicultural Research,* Vol. 18, no. 21 (1979), pp. 85–94.

INDEX

* indicates illustration